# Testimonials

"Dr. Richardson's book using Charlie the pot-bound plant as a metaphor for many of us as we live our lives is a gem. I plan to use it in my spiritual coaching practice and with my employees–helping them to examine how they are and are not nourishing themselves; where they have confined and constricted their ability to grow and expand and what to do about it. Charlie's life is also a great blueprint for me personally as I begin the next phase of my life."

Gerri H. Walker President/CEO
The Behavioral Health Center at Girard

"I found this book very easy to read. I love the metaphor the idea of being pot-bound as a plant. And, what you do to help that plant thrive including untangling all of the basis of the plant to enable yourself to look at life in a different way. I think that the metaphor is really spot on and I think the specificity is very helpful. I do believe that it provides lifelong lessons for anyone to take advantage of in a clear, concise fashion."

Deb Weinstein, VP
Human Resources GSK Oncology (retired)

"*Are You Pot-Bound*" is a short and sweet book for a common situation encountered by most career professionals: clients who are stuck in their lives and/or careers. Author Helen Richardson is wise, creative, and leads with her heart. She illustrates her plant metaphor with an adorable graphic and presents her content in the form of a workbook. The book is accessible, inspirational and full of meaningful insights."

**Kim Neubauer, Senior Career Consultant, U.S. Department of State, Drexel University LeBow College of Business and LHH**

"Dr. Richardson's metaphor of being 'pot-bound' beautifully highlights the importance of recognizing when we've outgrown our situations and need to seek new opportunities for growth. Pot-Bound' is a powerful guide for personal and professional growth. I highly recommend it to anyone feeling stuck or looking for a fresh perspective on their career or life journey."

**Joyel Crawford, Executive Success Coach and Fairygodmentor®**
**Crawford Leadership Strategies**

"The most powerful aspect of the book is its simplicity and the freedom it allows. Being able to follow the simplicity of the metaphor opened up a space for me to see the complexities of my life. Now in my current role, I'm able to use the metaphor of Charlie from the perspective of Helen being the owner of Charlie and being able to see and identify students that may be pot-bound, and how to help them either navigate it in the present or help them identify the markers of being pot-bound in the future, and how to make those transitions."

**Mr. Shontae Graham, MS, Ph.D candidate; Associate Director of Career Development, York College of Pennsylvania**

"I was Charlie too! After 25 years of very active ministry, I had outgrown my pot. My roots were overgrown and beginning to rot and I didn't even realize it until the Lord told me to step away and rest. I had neglected myself and my relationship with God. This book was another tool to open my eyes and get me on the right track."

**Kimberly Jones, President/Co-Founder, ereflow**

"For me, the Pot-Bound metaphor is all about self-awareness and self-care. Recognizing choice and freedom, and encouraging positive action, both for oneself as well as one's staff. I can easily imagine the Pot-Bound story being very helpful for people in the midst of a career transition, such as a promotion or a significant job change. It can help uncover even unconscious self-limiting beliefs that contribute to a feeling of stuckness, given its elegant simplicity, resonance and depth."

**Amanda Price, Communication and Conflict Skills Trainer, Coach, and Consultant**

# ARE YOU POT-BOUND?

Plant Wisdom for Getting Unstuck and Thriving in Life

Helen A. Richardson
EDD, PCC

*Are You Pot-Bound?: Plant Wisdom for Getting Unstuck and Thriving in Life*
©2024 by Helen A. Richardson, EdD, PCC
©2024 Career Consciousness

Published in United States by Skillbites LLC

Internet addresses given in this book were accurate at the time it went to press.

ISBN 978-1-952281-79-2 - paperback
ISBN 978-1-952281-80-8 - eBook

**All rights reserved.** No part of this publication may be reproduced or transmitted in any form or by any means, electronic or mechanical, including photocopying, recording, or any other information storage and retrieval system, without the written permission of the author or publisher.

**Printed in the United States of America**

For more information or to place bulk orders, contact the author or the publisher at info@skillbites.net.

Page 22 image © by kajani, image #624068476 - stockphoto.com
Author photo page 37 © Butler Prestige Photography
Charlie illustrations © Ryan Media, LLC

# DEDICATION

I dedicate this book to my loving and patient husband, Eugene, who has demonstrated what unconditional love looks like, and my caring and supportive children, Leon and Joey. Although they are pretty mature now, they can still fill my heart with joy and wonder much as they did when they were younger.

There is a sacred space in my heart for Giana and Aaron, my grandchildren. There is no better feeling of pure love than being a grandmother.

Of course, I cannot forget my eight brothers and sisters. Though five are gone, their legacy of love and light burns brightly inside me.

Last, but not least, I am forever grateful to my dad, Vernon Hemsley, the dreamer, and my mom, Anna Hemsley, the voice of wisdom and knowledge.

Yes, I feel love, love, love all around me.

# CONTENTS

Introduction ..................................................................... 9
Charlie's Story ................................................................ 13
Reflection ....................................................................... 23
How a Plant Becomes Pot-Bound ................................. 25
Are You Pot-Bound? ..................................................... 27
Points to Ponder – Part 1 .............................................. 29
Pot-Bound Playbook ..................................................... 31
Pot-Bound Prevention .................................................. 33
Points to Ponder – Part 2 .............................................. 35
Acknowledgments ......................................................... 37
About the Author .......................................................... 39

# Introduction

Hello! And thank you for picking up this book.

Let's start with a question: How often have you felt—or do you perhaps feel now—stuck or constrained because of the circumstances in your life? Or maybe you know someone, maybe a family member, colleague, coworker, or client, who feels this way. I call this feeling "pot-bound." Though I have accomplished many things in life—as I'm sure you have—I have become pot-bound at times, just like a plant when its pot is too small. For instance, in my work, I used to procrastinate getting things done because I wanted to make sure that they were just right. As a result, many projects were left half done, which detracted from my achieving my professional goals and made me feel like a failure. When I allowed myself to sit with the feelings of failure, I recognized that I had not failed but actually lacked focus. This awareness helped me to prioritize my work differently and get things done.

The book begins with the story of Charlie, my oldest living plant. One day, I noticed that Charlie, a 30-year-old snake plant, was pot-bound. Charlie's leaves were tight, wilting, and yellowing, signaling the plant's obvious distress. My experience restoring my beloved plant to its former healthy condition transformed both my personal and work life.

Charlie's story is uncomplicated and plainly worded, but it addresses more complex issues. Use it as a metaphor for your work and life and discover what you can learn from Charlie. Ask yourself, *In what ways have I become stuck, grown constrained, or outgrown my circumstances or "containers?"* And then, *In what ways could I be freed?*

Charlie's story is followed by sections for reflections and points to ponder, along with a pot-bound quiz. The point of this book is to be a guide to uncovering your strengths, goals, and purpose. I have benefitted from the Charlie metaphor, and have used it with other individuals and groups from all backgrounds and generations. Many of them have benefitted from an insight or an "aha" moment that helped them make a meaningful shift.

While the book will be helpful for the individual reader, I believe it will be of greatest benefit when facilitated in a group setting. Below are testimonials from pot-bound workshops.

> "Dr. Richardson's workshop was very insightful to me. I learned a lot about the impact that my career can have on my personal life and vice versa. One big takeaway was that often it's not that you can't grow and flourish, but you may just need a new perspective on your purpose."

> "The workshop allowed me to reflect on what my personal values are and how they have been a part of my professional life. The story helped me realize how I was able to grow and learn from my past experiences and navigate them better. Additionally, being able to clarify what brings me peace in my personal and professional life has been an important part of my well-being."

## Introduction

*"I wish I had taken Dr. Richardson's workshop much earlier in my career. The ideas of thinking about what one needs, how to nourish oneself, and what one wants, and then aligning those bits to one's career can be a very powerful framework. Bottom line is that melding work with personal goals and values can be challenging, however, in the end, it's very rewarding holistically."*

*"For me, the Pot-Bound experience is all about self-awareness and self-care. Recognizing choice and freedom, and encouraging positive action, both for oneself as well as one's staff."*

*"Sometimes we feel alone, and we are not; this was validating, empowering."*

Consider contacting me, Dr. Helen Richardson, to facilitate a life-changing conversation at your school, workplace, community of faith, governmental facility, healthcare, and senior living spaces. Career coaches, organization development consultants, and human resource professionals will also find this book a great resource to use with their clients.

Please contact me through my website, www.careerc.com, where you will find more information about the workshops. You will also find information for coaches and skilled facilitators on how to use the workshop with your new and existing clients. I look forward to hearing from you.

Now let's meet Charlie.

# Charlie's Story

The story of Charlie, the snake plant and how he transformed my life, started on a Saturday afternoon in 2021.

When I first got Charlie, he was a small, six-inch plant in a dish garden within a cluster of peace lilies, jades, and philodendrons. It was given to me as gift when I was in my first marriage many years ago. The other plants in the dish garden died, but Charlie survived.

From that very young plant in a dish garden, Charlie is now about three feet tall with a canopy that is two feet wide.

Over the 30 years, Charlie was moved to many environments. He was potted and repotted and loved. His long leaves were sometimes squished in a car, moving van in snow and rain. Charlie was always a survivor.

## Are You Pot-Bound?

This special Saturday, as I was preparing my home for guests on Sunday, I *really* looked at Charlie for the first time in a long time. I realized that Charlie had not been consuming much water for several months and saw that his leaves had started to droop. Snake plants are very hardy, and they need very little care.

They can appear healthy even when they may not be. I knew that Charlie had always been a survivor, so I focused on my other plants and put Charlie in the background. This day, it finally hit me: Charlie was dying.

*Charlie's Story*

*Are You Pot-Bound?*

I stared at Charlie and became very saddened by how he looked.

I frantically asked my husband to help me tie his leaves together so that he could stand tall, the way he once did. Yet, this made Charlie appear even sadder. My Charlie was really looking his age.

"Charlie has to go. He's dead," I said to my husband, and I began to cry.

*Charlie's Story*

*How can I throw him away? It's my fault he looks like this. Why didn't I do something before he became so frail?* I wondered. To my great surprise, I became overwhelmed with emotion. Somehow, I connected Charlie to me. Then I knew: *I had to save him.*

As I continued to stare at him, I realized that Charlie looked the way he did and was dying because he was pot-bound. I immediately found a larger pot and some fresh dirt and repotted Charlie. I gave him some water, and within five minutes his drooping leaves began to stand up. My Charlie came back to life. I knew that the world was not done with Charlie yet!

# Reflection

Reflect on my story and how the story translates to your life or your purpose for being. I think Charlie's story is a metaphor for life.

We are our own caretakers, yet at times, we become pot-bound, unable to sustain ourselves from within. We have taken all the nourishment we can from our current environment—our friends, family, relationships, school, and jobs.

It's then that we need larger pots. We need new dirt. We need fresh water. We need to breathe pure air. We need to know how to survive in the various temperatures of our lives. Most of all, we need to monitor ourselves so that we don't become so complacent with our lives that we fall into a near-death state.

> **Most of all, we need to monitor ourselves so that we don't become so complacent with our lives that we fall into a near-death state.**

Charlie was silent—much like the parts of ourselves that we ignore. *Or… are they actually trying to speak, but we don't listen to them and then wonder what has happened to us?*

When I look further into what this story means to me, I conceptualize its parts this way.

> **The pot** represents my strengths and culture. It is the meaning, goals, and purpose for my life. It's the container that holds me together. It's my safe place, and it protects me.

*Reflection*

**The dirt** is my personal and professional life. The seed that became the plant represents the ideas that have been planted in me, the messages I have digested and swallowed. It's my beliefs, choices, fears, hopes, and expectations.

**The roots** of the plant are my relationships, those connections that are so core to my being. They anchor me. The roots are also my spiritual values, those ideals that matter most to me.

**The leaves** are my life energy. They are my way of monitoring how I feel about my work and life—sick or well— and it is my way of giving myself water and needed sun. They are my way of knowing when I need to revitalize my precious energy through mindfulness, meditation, exercise, and prayer. When re-energized, I feel peaceful, I recognize my potential, and I am able to make good choices.

So, as you work with this metaphor, I invite you to use my way of conceptualizing what this story means to you, or develop your own.

# How a Plant Becomes Pot-Bound

Pot-bound plants are those that have outgrown their containers. If you've ever bought a plant in a garden center and found a solid tangle of roots when you took it out of the container, you are familiar with the problem.

Plants by nature are meant to be grown outdoors. As an outdoor plant grows full and leafy above the ground, down below, its roots grow downward and outward. Ideally, there is unlimited room for the roots to spread out in search of moisture and nutrients.

Whenever we take a plant and put it into a container, we're taking matters into our own hands. Plants become dependent on us for the right soil and light exposure, nutrients, sufficient water, and drainage. While things may look good at the start, it's what we don't see below the soil level that may undo our good intentions.

The problem is this: whenever we put a plant into a container, we limit the amount of space its roots have to grow and spread.

As the plant matures, its developing roots run out of space to expand down and out, and will instead begin to wrap themselves in overlapping circles around the inner walls of the pot. A plant whose roots are bound by some kind of barrier is a pot-bound— or root-bound—plant.

> **While things may look good at the start, it's what we don't see below the soil level that may undo our good intentions.**

*How a Plant Becomes Pot-Bound*

It's hardly healthy for the plant, because when there are more roots than soil in a pot, there won't be enough nutrients left for the plant to continue to grow. Leaves may turn yellow and begin to wilt. And, when roots become packed, water isn't absorbed effectively, leading to wilting leaves on a thirsty plant. Left unaddressed, the situation can ultimately lead to the plant's demise.

# Are You Pot-Bound?

Answer "yes" or "no" to the following:

1. Do you feel trapped by your current situation? This could be a job, relationship, or living situation.  _____

2. Do you experience frustration, boredom, and lack of growth? Have these states of mind become your constant companions?  _____

3. Have your friends and family suggested that they experience you differently—that you are lacking the energy and vitality you once had?  _____

4. Are you noticing that your ability to adapt to new things, circumstances, and opportunities is now more troublesome for you than it once was? Are your private thoughts fixated on fear of failure, risk avoidance, and resistance to change?  _____

5. Are you feeling somewhat suffocated by your tangled network of habits, routines, or obligations that limit your freedom and creativity?  _____

## *Are You Pot-Bound?*

6. Are you feeling overwhelmed, stressed, or exhausted? This may show up in how you look, a change in your desire for exercise, and greater difficulty waking up in the morning.   _____

7. Are you aware of a shift in your mood based upon the weather or the people you are with? Does it stifle your energy?   _____

8. Are you stuck in the past, constantly rewriting your life with "what-ifs?"   _____

9. Have you limited your network of friends?   _____

10. Are you consumed with the desire to move somewhere else?   _____

**1 to 3 "yes" responses:** *You might be pot-bound.*
**4 to 6 "yes" responses:** *You are likely pot-bound.*
**7 to 10 "yes" responses:** *You need a new pot!*

# Points to Ponder - Part 1

1. What is your pot—your strengths and culture, your meaning, goals, and purpose? Where do you feel most safe?

_____
_____
_____

2. At an early age, what nourishment (or lack thereof) did "the dirt in your pot" give you that has impacted your personal and professional life?

_____
_____
_____

3. What "seeds" were planted in you? As you grew up, what messages about yourself did you digest without even thinking?

_____
_____
_____

4. Throughout your life, what messages, relationships, and situations clogged you up and turned your leaves brown?

_____
_____
_____

5. What are your roots—the things that hold the most meaning for you? What anchors you?

_____
_____
_____

6. Who were the people and situations that nourished you—the way the sunlight, plant food, and water nourish a plant?

_____
_____
_____

# Pot-Bound Playbook

If you are pot-bound, see how this strategy might work for you.

- Think about some of your old visions for your life. **Dig deep for those old dreams** that you placed in some corner of your mind and find them buried in your heart. Maybe they are there because you didn't believe it was possible for you because of your age, sex, sexual orientation, race, disability, etc.

- **Pull up those visions** for yourself and allow the anger, resentment, and rage to come to the surface. Inspect each root emotion and consider how the anger, resentment, and other negative emotions have stunted your growth and drained your energy. Forgive yourself and now begin to let it go. **Close your eyes, visualize your dream, and feel what it feels like to be repotted, and all those negative parts are just pruned away.**

- **Determine the one or two things that you feel are critical for enhancing the quality of your work and life.** Write it/them down with five clear action steps and take your first step. Share your new life idea with a friend and ask them to be your accountability partner.

- Now take yourself to your new place and try on the feeling of contentment with yourself. You are now where you want to be.

- You have given yourself some new dirt, and changed your environment; if not physically, then certainly mentally.

- **The old pot is broken.** You have a bigger one where you can continue to explore and find new challenges and possibilities.

- You are in sync with what your body needs regarding water, sun, and food.

- You are out in the air and becoming what you want to be. With regular monitoring of the temperatures of your life, you will know what you need to bring your desires into reality. Learn to meditate or if you know how, make it a part of the structure of your life.

- Repeat this process whenever you feel stuck.

# Pot-Bound Prevention

There are three basic ways to avoid becoming pot-bound: ***container selection, repotting, and pruning***. As with a plant, you need to have enough space for the opportunities to grow and continue to develop.

1. **Container selection**

    Just as plants need a pot that matches their size and requirements, you require an environment that supports your goals and aspirations.

    For example, this could be your home, workplace, community, or country. If you are beginning to feel that your current container is too small or limiting, consider moving to a different one, where you will have ample room and resources where you can thrive.

2. **Repotting**

    Consider repotting on a regular basis. Even if you have a suitable container now, as you learn new skills over time, and have new experiences, and achieve new milestones, you might outgrow it. To prevent becoming pot-bound, contemplate repotting. You will change your situation, feel like a "new birth" to take on new challenges and pursue new opportunities. With repotting, you'll have a refreshing perspective, stimulate your creativity, and greatly expand your horizons.

3. **Pruning**

   Clutter is the culprit, because sometimes, becoming pot-bound is not a result of having too little space, but having too much clutter, so consider pruning occasionally. There might be accumulated habits, routines, obligations, or relationships that are no longer serving you or holding you back from reaching your potential. Pot-bound avoidance can be accomplished by letting go of what is no longer useful or beneficial for you. By pruning what is no longer useful, you free up space and provide room for you to focus on what matters most.

# Points to Ponder - Part 2

1. Are there new seeds that you would like to plant to nurture more of what you want for your life and work?

_____
_____
_____

2. Do you have any brown leaves that you need to pluck off and discard?

_____
_____
_____

3. Do you need to assess your roots and any entanglements there—things to separate from and establish boundaries with?

_____
_____
_____

4. Are there parts of your life that you want to give away to make room in your pot?

_____
_____
_____

5. Which parts of yourself should you give away to share your love and grow your legacy?

___

___

___

# Acknowledgments

I am grateful for the guidance of my early mentors, Della Clark and Matt Bergheiser at The Enterprise Center in Philadelphia. They helped me to know that I had something meaningful with the ideas and approach of Career Consciousness.

Tim Styer of Ride to Work, Sheila Ireland of Philadelphia OIC, and Donna Cooper of Children First were some of my first clients in workforce and career development training. They provided me the opportunity to make a difference with what could be considered challenging populations. My approach significantly improved the career trajectory of training participants, leading to better work habits, several promotions, higher retention levels, and significant numbers of people returning to school.

None of my early work would have been possible without the energy, imagination, and "can-do" spirit of my loyal lieutenant, Dr. Germaine Edwards.

While many training sessions were done with experienced trainers, it was Dolores Davis and her amazing facilitation skills that made people call us the "Dynamic Duo."

Finally, I want to thank Rosalind Spigel and Alexis Jackson, who provided the initial recruitment and technology for the four pilot focus groups that

*Acknowledgments*

were conducted with individuals from four generations. The 28 participants in the pilot groups who read the Charlie Story and participated in workshops let me know that the simple metaphor was an opening for meaningful shifts in perspective. Their input made this book a must-have for Career Consciousness.

# About the Author

Dr. Helen Richardson
Career and Executive Coach -
Cultivating Growth Through Metaphor

As a young child, my connection to plants was always there. While my brothers and sisters laughed and called me "weird" for talking and singing to morning glories and marigolds in our small North Philadelphia backyard, I found happiness among the greenery. Plants, with their quiet life force, always brought me joy.

As I matured, my bond with plants continued. When I acquired indoor plants, each new addition received a name—often after a departed sibling—turning my home into a place of living memories. I lovingly cared for them, referring to plants as my "babies."

However, my journey extended beyond the garden. I am Dr. Helen Richardson, Founder and CEO of Career Consciousness, Inc. With over 35 years of experience in human resources, career coaching, and workforce development, I've dedicated my professional life to helping others thrive. My path was shaped by early experiences as an 18-year-old mother, the youngest of nine children, and a woman with North Philadelphia roots. I discovered that happiness at home is complicated, and most times tied to contentment at work and vice versa—a revelation that fuels my purpose.

I am recognized as a career thought leader—a "work sage," who has developed two transformative career development models: "A New Way to Think About Work®" for adults and "Find Your Wings®" for youth. My academic background includes a doctorate in organizational development and training from Temple University, a Masters in Human Services from Lincoln University, and professional coaching certification from the International Coaching Federation (ICF).

My greatest successes lie in coaching diverse populations: from welfare-to-work individuals to apprenticeship students and government workers seeking renewed purpose. My personal mission is simple yet profound: ***I see talent in all people. I see dignity in all work. I join with others to make visible the oak tree within the acorn.***

And yes, even as a coach, I experienced my own moments of being "pot-bound", the transformative encounter with Charlie—the plant inspired me to write this book. Through Charlie's story, I hope to guide others toward growth, renewal, and the realization that we, too, can break free from our constraints.

Thank you for joining me on this journey of metaphorical growth and discovery.

The real Charlie.

www.ingramcontent.com/pod-product-compliance
Lightning Source LLC
Chambersburg PA
CBHW050047080526
**44586CB00014B/1498**